THE SKILL OF SELLING ONLINE:

Persuade the hardest prospective client and gain new prospects

Michael Green

Table of Contents

Chapter 1: The Selling Process

Imagine a series of tiny booths on the sandy road somewhere in the Middle East, many hundred years ago. The booths sit side-by-side on both sides of a dusty roadway. Others individuals in the throng are merely travelling from one location to another, while some have come to acquire a specific thing. The sellers utilize all kinds of tactics and techniques to capture the attention of the pedestrians and pull them to their own booth rather than to their neighbor's.

Each seller must persuade one individual at a time that he has the greatest goods compared to all others around him and that it would be a catastrophic error to purchase from anybody else but him. The buyer needs to be persuaded that what he is giving up is nothing in exchange for the value that he is obtaining in return.

This is the art of selling.

Every business operator, whether on a dusty street in the Middle East or in an air-conditioned high-rise in New York City, needs to persuade the buyer that his product is the greatest and that the customer would be losing out on a wonderful bargain by walking away from the transaction. The purpose of the individual or corporation selling the products and services is to persuade the customer that he will gain more than he is being asked to give.

People have been perfecting the art of selling things and services to people who need them since the dawn of time. The techniques that entrepreneurs use to market their products have evolved through through the millennia, but the concepts are essentially the same.

No company exists without a buyer.

No transaction occurs unless a buyer is satisfied that he will profit by making the purchase. The buyer needs to feel that what he is giving up in exchange is worth less than what he is gaining. An individual who enters into a fast food restaurant appreciates the meal more than the few bucks that the meal will cost. If the buyer doesn't think that he is receiving more than he's providing, there is no transaction.

Selling online is no different.

Granted, the way of selling online is very new in the history of commerce, and there are some specific strengths and disadvantages associated with online commerce that did not come into play only a few years ago. Selling online is still selling, and the basics have stayed intact down through decades of economic transactions.

One of the main concerns about internet vendors is that the overwhelming majority of them appear to focus exclusively about completing the deal.

Since of the ubiquitous reach of the Internet, it's easy for some online vendors to believe they can hide because they're not starting the consumer eye-to-eye across a counter in a physical store. Buyers may also feel less safe since they can't meet the vendor face-to-face, and they normally cannot visit the shop in person and convince themselves of the legality of the firm.

These dishonest internet vendors actually have little concern for the client; they value only what the customer can do for them, which is contributing cash to their bank account. It is extremely easy for an internet vendor to develop an entire business strategy on one-time transactions rather than creating a list of delighted consumers who come back for recurring purchases.

That's the risk awaiting internet merchants
— the bad reputation of a few.

Other internet retailers — the sort you want
to be – couldn't be more different. They
truly do want to do the right thing, and
they're cognizant of the need to deliver
honest value to their consumers. Their
objective is to deliver great value to the
consumer at a reasonable price, but they
occasionally struggle to articulate that value.
Their heart is in the right place, but they
have problems reaching out and persuading
the consumer that they're different from the
other group. No company can flourish
without a sale enticing a customer to pay.

Even if your heart is in the right place, you'll
have to master the skill of persuading others
that you have what they need if you want to
thrive in your internet company. People
using the Internet nowadays have the
attention span of Middle Eastern consumers

passing along a dusty street, hardly looking at the sellers who plead for their attention.

Online vendors must attract the attention of prospective consumers and persuade them that the things they are offering genuinely can help them solve their issues and can do it better and cheaper than anyone else's product can. What you are selling simply must be better, and you must also think that it is better and be able to articulate that.

Whatever your goods or service, you must be able to persuade the consumer that what he gives up in exchange is less than the value he's obtaining by making a purchase from your online business.
It's your responsibility to create the demand, or at least to amplify it, so that you're standing ready with your product or service just as soon as the consumer is sure of his need.

Chapter 2: Show Customers the Value

A well-known saying goes like this: "I don't mind purchasing; I simply don't enjoy being marketed." That term rings true for a lot of Internet customers. They don't mind spending more, even high-ticket things, provided they believe they are receiving more value than they're giving up. Whether it's $5, $500, or $5000, there's a customer at each one of those price points if you, the vendor, can persuade him that he will receive at least double his money back from the transaction.

It's not the monetary amount per se; it's the amount of projected return.

It's not about selling cheap, low-ticket products but about understanding that customers always want more than they're ready to offer.

You have to demonstrate to them very clearly the value of what you're delivering. It's the traditional contrast between features and benefits. Features are things that a product can accomplish, but benefits are what those features can do for the consumer. You need to emphasize on the advantage to the consumer by highlighting precisely what the buyer will be able to gain by acquiring your goods.

Today's Internet buyers are knowledgeable and suspicious. They've seen all sorts of gimmicks and frauds and may have lost money in the past. With such a high degree of suspicion, Internet shoppers nowadays must grasp fully what the product can achieve for them before they are prepared to whip out their credit card.

There must be a suitable fit between the values the product is delivering and the price that buyers are being asked to pay. If there's too much of a gap between the two, purchasers will be skeptical. They'll assume either that you're attempting to con them if the price is too high, or that there must be a gimmick if the price is too low. You can't really blame them, since there are many Internet marketers that are adopting all sorts of unscrupulous techniques merely to persuade the consumer to click on the Buy Now button.

But you've already determined that you're going to be different — that's fantastic.

What can you do to assist consumers grasp the value in your product?

1. Show the value. This is the point we've been discussing. You must restate the advantages of your product so that the consumer starts to connect those benefits with your offering. Use every platform available: affiliate advertisements, banner

ads, pay-per-click click campaigns, even classified ads. Your aim is that your product becomes associated with the advantages that it delivers the consumer. When the consumer thinks of a certain issue, you want him to think of your product as the sole solution for that problem.

2. Be distinctive. The marketplace today is inundated with items competing with yours, many of which are practically identical. What can you do to make your product stand out? You have to identify something about your product which is novel or distinctive. People are highly interested in the newest stuff. No one is interested in last year's model, whether it's a mobile phone, a DVD player, or auto. People don't want mediocre things, and they don't want obsolete items. They want the newest product so they can show their buddies and boast on the fantastic price they obtained. You need to be aware of this propensity and advertise toward it. If you believe you

should be subtle, don't. Be bold and forthright. Make sure the consumer understands what you have to offer compared to all the other items which appear extremely similar.

3. Offer a guarantee. Yes, it's true that some scam artists would place a "Satisfaction Guaranteed" graphic on their website with no intention whatsoever of providing money back to disappointed clients, much less returning an email from a frustrated customer. We've already concluded that you are dedicated to being a new sort of web marketer.

Giving a money-back guarantee provides the consumer a feeling of comfort while buying on your website. If you're afraid to issue a complete money-back guarantee, try a free trial version with an expiry date, or a basic model with an opportunity to upgrade later to a premium one if the consumer is happy. The important aspect is that the consumer needs to be persuaded that you stand behind your goods.

4. Be honest. There's just no alternative way to explain this. It's true that every salesman is devoted to amplifying the advantages of this product and reducing drawbacks. No one is asking you to do anything different. You must believe in the worth of your product and be able to convey that value to the consumer. There are so many fly-by-night websites that make all kinds of claims and then disappear after a short period of selling online.

The famous golden rule is one of the finest rules for this part of your business: treat people as you would like to be treated. And it's also crucial to remember that individuals talk more freely on the Internet about the experiences they've had. You want to do everything you can to preserve your internet reputation. The last thing you want is blog postings and forum comments with regularly unfavorable remarks about your product. That's death to an internet company. Be honest, be proud of your product, and be genuine about what it can and can't accomplish. You may lose some sales in the near term, but in the long run your firm will be built on a more stable basis.

Chapter 3: Be Authentic, Responsive, and Real

One of Henry Ford's famous comments is, "People may purchase the Model T in whatever color they like, as long as it's black." As any vehicle salesperson will tell you now, the days of people taking what they are promised are long gone. Buyers are fussy, they want what they want, and they don't enjoy being told what they can or can't acquire. The days of churning out goods without care for the interests of the consumer will never return. Online purchasers that are flourishing nowadays provide a broad selection of alternatives or even customised items.

People want items tailored for them, and the more unique, the better.

Any great salesman understands that creating a connection initially is a major benefit, both in completing the purchase and in generating future business. In the same manner, an internet marketer must allow his own personality to show through. You just cannot hide behind the pages of your website. Companies that are thriving in selling online display a human touch in a number of ways.

Here are a just a few examples:
• Auto-responders enable firms to customize emails, utilizing the initial name of a prospective customer and making the\semail seem as if it were written only for that buyer.

• A money-back promise that is personally guaranteed by the seller's name and even an image may be a very strong weapon for preventing buyer's regret. People want to know that they're dealing with a human, and that person stands behind the goods.

• Blogs are one of the finest methods for showcasing your personal side. Customers prefer engaging with the seller, before and after the transaction, so that they know they can obtain support if they need it, and they won't be left out in the cold.

• Successful internet merchants have 24/7 support services for their clientele. Many consumers who purchase online are doing it from a different time zone than the vendor, or late at night, long after brick-and-mortar companies have closed their doors for the evening. Customers need to know that they can access help at any moment.

• Interactive surveys, particularly in combination with a free gift, offer a terrific approach for firms to communicate on the personal level with their clients. The poll findings also provide vital market research, so that firms may focus their offers to the ever-changing demands of the customer.

• It's crucial that there exist items in various pricing levels, whether you are selling products or services. Sometimes a consumer merely wants to test the quality of your product without committing to a higher priced item, and some customers just don't have a lot of money to spend at this moment. By giving cheaper cost things, you may give them a taste for the product and for the way the firm interacts with its clients. Many of these clients who arrived at a low price point will upgrade and remain with the firm long-term, and they're delighted with the care they've been provided.

The days of the black Model T are long gone. Customization, personalisation, and flexibility are the name of the game.
You need to be authentic, visible, and available if you want to flourish online.

Chapter 4: Lead; Don't Sell

People automatically desire to purchase from the merchant who's top in class. Only in rare cases can customers gravitate toward a firm in second or third position. Granted, every corporation would want to think of itself as being in first position, but statistically and objectively, that's simply not true. There is a reason why brand names dominate over the globe, whether soft drinks, movies, music, apparel, etc. People are prepared to pay a premium for the brand name, and that's simply because of perceived quality.

Quality is a given with market leaders.
Your aim as an online seller is not to sell per se but to expand your firm into the market leading position. You need to dominate your area and establish your brand name such that it's known as a leader. When things go tight, as they are today, people flock around

leaders, not ready to risk their money for a product that may be of poorer quality, even if the price is greater.

So have you gained market domination as a leader in your niche?

1. You must be visible. As we stated earlier, you are your brand name. Your own name recognition is vital for domination in your area. There are various methods to achieve this, but one of the most crucial is to get your name out there and visible on the Internet. You may conduct collaborative partnerships with other marketers, even rivals in some cases. There's no ban prohibiting print advertising, such as magazine or newspaper adverts. The pay-per-click campaign, handled successfully, may be vital in developing your brand name awareness.

Even if visitors don't click through on the link, they continue seeing your name over and over again on numerous sites they visit. One fascinating technique many web marketers don't think about is establishing an affiliate campaign. If you have affiliates that are rewarded for selling your product, then they have every reason to spread your brand in as many areas as they can. While you may give up part of your income since you have to compensate the affiliates, what generally occurs if the affiliate marketing campaign is done properly, is that your firm gathers momentum and starts to develop tremendously.

2. Establish your authority. You must be regarded as the "go to" person in your field. People immediately trust and heed counsel from authoritative persons. There are various ways to establish oneself in this position, and some of the more well-known approaches include article writing, forum posting, and producing e-books. Each of these tactics will add to your authority as

time goes by and more and more people get acquainted with the quality of your work.

3. Polish your blog. Your blog is the one area where current and future consumers can hear your actual voice. Put your photo on your blog. Talk about your life. You are not compelled to divulge everything about yourself, but blogging provides your readers a sense of who you are as a person. Then, when you need to talk like an authority, people will be more inclined to accept what you say. Of course, we should remind out that authority once again may be swiftly lost owing to poor writing or factual inaccuracies. Pause and ponder before you publish each and every post.

Think about persons in your own life who are authority figures for you. Why do you consider them as an authority? Most likely, it's a matter of knowledge, experience, wisdom, and that gut-level sense of knowing what to do and what not to do. The same concepts will remain true in Internet marketing; you just utilize other methods to get to the same objective.

Building your authority requires time and work.

While there are numerous firms that claim to offer a shortcut to establishing your authority, there truly is no better approach than the old-fashioned manner. You must become renowned for constant, persistent, and trustworthy material of the highest quality that genuinely benefits people.

Chapter 5: Take Advantage of Social Networking

Internet marketing is all about people. Social networking is a terrific method for individuals to remain in contact, and it is still the most popular tool for friends to connect with friends. The three biggest social networking sites are by now known to practically everyone online: creating a connection initially is a huge benefit, both in completing the transaction and in generating future business.

In addition, additional sites are going online and rising in popularity every day. It's crucial to remember why individuals use social networking sites. It's to stay in touch with friends. You need to keep this in mind when you think about your Internet marketing plan. If you have ever had a friend or family member who was active in network marketing, then you are aware of the obstacles. Have you ever had to break off all communication with some "friends" because they just could not quit talking about their "opportunity"? Their failure to switch off the business spiel may eventually cost them the connection. That's the last thing you want to happen to you in your social networking effort.

While it's true that people come to your site with the expectation that you are selling things, you need to discover the fine balance between being a useful resource and monetizing your social networking sites. This balance may fluctuate based on the sort of company that you run. But the essential thing to ask yourself is, "Would I like to visit my site?" That's a hard question to answer. But you have to beg for it. It's crucial to remember the fundamentals. People prefer to get out with their buddies. They prefer to purchase, but not to be sold. Keep these guidelines in mind as you create your social networking approach. Establish a Long-Term Relationship Through Email Marketing

From a cost standpoint, email marketing provides a fantastic boost to the bottom line. In the recent past, firms had to pay for printing, paper, and postage to keep in contact with their consumers. And don't be deceived: off-line mail-order is alive and well today, and there is a place for off-line marketing when planning the long-term strategy of your online company. But, in particular, email marketing is highly effective when done properly. There's a reason why people disregard most of their emails: they receive too much spam.

Emails being caught in the spam folder is the death knell for an email marketing campaign. Also, sending spam emails might be the death blow to your financial bottom line. With U.S. government legislation raising the punishment for Internet marketers who send unsolicited emails, the danger is simply too great for your online company to overlook compliance with this new rule.

At least, you should utilize your autoresponder program to guarantee that everyone getting your emails has opted in freely. If you would like to learn more about the penalties for Internet marketers that send unsolicited emails, go to www.fcc.gov/guides/spam-unwanted-text-messages-and-email for more information. As far as email marketing is concerned, you want to remember that the fundamental aim is to establish connections with your clients for the long term. Your objective is not to develop a list of hundreds of thousands of individuals who couldn't care less about your company. Your objective is to remain in contact with your client base and give the latest news about your goods and services to clients who may be interested.

With those aims in mind, here are some pointers on how to develop an efficient email marketing campaign:

1. First impressions are important. Craft your first email extremely carefully. Sign up to get your own email and check your message as it arrives in your own mailbox. How does it look? If you were an uninterested consumer, would you click on it? Because your first email will follow quickly after the buyer opts into your list, the likelihood that they will read it is high. However, you simply must capture their attention in this initial email and supply them with exceptional content, or they'll probably never read another email from you again.

2. Make sure the quality of the materials remains good. People read emails in order to gain information and learn things that will aid them in their everyday lives or enterprises. They do not read emails to be marketed to. Be careful to deliver

good-quality information so people truly look forward to receiving your emails. Use subheadings, bulleted lists, and short paragraphs to break up the text and make it more readable.

3. Be cautious not to elevate the reader's expectations too high. The goal is that you will be sending them plenty of emails, so don't set a standard for yourself that you can't meet. It's better to under promise and over deliver than to have one fantastic email followed by a succession of mediocre ones.

4. Try to offer value with every email, even if it means giving away something for free. The free item doesn't have to cost you anything. It might be anything that you've learnt from your experience, like an excellent website, a free report, or a discount for future purchases. Remember that everything related to you and your company, even if it's free, needs to be of the utmost value.

5. Entice individuals to communicate with you in the body of the email. Use hyperlinks and HTML buttons to persuade users to go over to your website.

6. Put in extra effort on the email's subject line.Be mindful of the look of the email on the numerous tools that people use to explore the Internet, such as smartphones and other portable devices. Your headline must capture their attention within the first few words. Make sure that you express in the headline of the email why they really must open your email and read your content.

Think about emails that you appreciate receiving. Do you look forward to receiving emails from a certain business? If so, why? Is there anything you can learn from that company to help you start your own?Think about what you appreciate as a consumer, and attempt to walk in your customer's shoes while designing your email campaign. Your aim is to make your consumers look forward to receiving your next email and open it the first time. It's all about the long-term partnership.

Chapter 6:   Reassure Your Customers

Consumers are naturally nervous after acquiring goods. They worry that they've spent money in vain, spent too much money, or behaved recklessly. Your mission is to erase this buyer's regret as fast and fully as feasible. Depending on the sort of product or service you're offering, it's highly probable that consumers may have some inquiries regarding it. If it's software, they'll have difficulty installing it. If it's an ebook, they'll have questions about particular passages. Whatever product or service you have, people have questions about it. You need to be there for them through this first inquiry in order to create trust and have a shot at future purchases. There's nothing more annoying than an online firm that vanishes after the transaction. If you have software to run your help desk, make sure it works at all times and that consumers receive rapid solutions to their inquiries. An excellent suggestion is to send an automated message as soon as the individual has filed a request, verifying that the request has been received and will be answered shortly.

If your product is a little sophisticated, you may wish to give a video lesson describing how to utilize it. This might be on your thank you page when the money is received. On the same download page, you should offer comprehensive contact information on how to reach your firm in case there are queries or problems.

This is the one moment at which you want to make yourself the most approachable, since your customer has just bought a product from you and doesn't know you that well. You need to prove that you are entirely dedicated to giving service after the sale. If you're selling tangible things, you could sneak in a CD or DVD at absolutely no extra expense. Another suggestion is to send a follow-up email, or maybe a phone call, after a few days to make sure that the individual has not had any difficulties with the goods. This follow-up will gain you respect and appreciation and, in nearly all situations, will lead to a long-term connection with your new client.

Chapter 7: Take the Lead in Your Niche

The Internet is a busy environment, and competition is severe. Visitors to your website owe you nothing because of the time you spent creating your company. The most you can expect to obtain is a few seconds of their attention before they go on to the next site. During those few seconds, you must immediately show how you are superior to the competitors.

Despite numerous instances to the contrary, the greatest technique to attract the reader's attention is not by employing flashing arrows or garish images. The sort of consumer you'll attract by being flashy will not remain with you in the long term; it's just a matter of time before someone else comes up with a flashier website. The best way to obtain a permanent advantage over your competitors is by giving great information and taking care of your consumers.

Here are a few suggestions to help you think about your website and how you can break away from the pack and grab the lead:

1.You must show at all times that you deserve to be the best website in your field. There should be no question in the market that you are the best at what you do. At no time can you let customers' expectations fall short. Spread the word in as many areas online as possible since you can answer questions on blogs and forums and always reply to enquiries from consumers. This process may take time, but you'll find yourself just a notch above your competitors, and that's where you need to be.

2. Have a clear pricing strategy.Simply placing a $47 price tag on an e-book doesn't guarantee that it's worth that price, and you

might progressively drive yourself out of business by undercutting your competitors and giving a lower price than everyone else. Your objective is to get a fair price for fair goods. You want clients who downloaded your goods or bought your services to be happy with the value they received for the money they paid. If your pricing is below your competition's, then there should be a compelling business rationale to do so. If your prices are greater than those of your competitors, then you must give more value. It's all about delivering on your commitments.

3. Keep in mind, your website is not a passive, static cash generator. You need to put out new versions of your items regularly and keep researching better methods to enhance them. Experiment with split testing, conduct time-definite promotions, and provide free samples to evaluate market demand, etc., to think about new methods to sell your items and manage your firm.

Internet marketing is continuously developing, and so must your company.

4. Remember that it's more costly to attract a customer than to maintain one. Never underestimate the significance of a returning client. Take excellent care of everyone who's bought your items or services. Be sensitive to client complaints, and be fast to handle issues and problems. Remember that your consumers don't know you; they don't know what a fantastic person you are. You have to show it by your attentiveness to their demands.

You must always fulfill your money-back promises precisely as you said you would: without difficulty, without inquiry, without delay. Your aim is to respond to all support requests, whether based on customer service or technical concerns, within 24 hours. You'd expect no less yourself, if you were the consumer.

5. Be in touch with what your consumers' desire. Check out blogs, forums, and other websites to see what people are asking for. It's not that you push your favorite items on them. Rather, you concentrate on what consumers desire and offer it to them. Don't be frightened of your unborn from time to time. If you've done something amazing to improve a product, dubbed "say so," Customers are watching, and when they realize that you have integrated one of their recommendations into your next product, you'll gain their respect and their continued business.

6. Know your competitors' This is true for every company, whether you are selling doughnuts, dry cleaning, or computers. At no time can you be taken by surprise. Sign up for your competitors' newsletters, monitor their marketing methods, and see if there are techniques that you can use. Be aware of what is going on around you so you can measure your response to customers'

requirements and if you need to go in a
particular way.

Chapter 8: Be Honest

The finest salesmen and saleswomen down through the centuries have spoken the truth. However, there's nothing at all wrong with an element of spin; to sell a product, you must emphasise the advantages. The selling is all about ethics and honesty. The old days of customers taking whatever they got from the corporation are giving way to online evaluations on third-party websites, where people hold companies to account and are quick to call out product faults and flaws. You do not want to be on the wrong end of such reviews. You want consumers praising your goods, and to achieve that, you have to be upfront about what you will and won't do.

Customers expect you to sell to them. They expect to pay a fair price for a fair product; therefore, they don't mind entering into the transaction with the knowledge that your organization exists to sell items. There are selling tactics that follow in the field of ethical selling. Consumers expect to see them, and it's not a breach of ethics to attempt to sell as best you can.

An excellent example is what's generally termed "up-selling. If you were asked "Would you want fries with that?" in a fast food restaurant, it is a basic example of up-selling. If a consumer buys a product and sometimes throughout the selling process you offer another product that is somewhat more costly but has more advantages, there's no ethical problem with reminding a customer of another product that you have that could satisfy his needs better, even if the cost is greater. If you think that your product genuinely helps address consumer issues, then there's no breach of conscience in selling another product that you have in addition to the one that the client has just purchased.

In the same manner, it's entirely ethical to down-sell or give a consumer a terrific discount once they've denied your original offer. Suppose that the individual is interested in your items but is not interested in spending the money. Is there anything you could offer that would meet their needs while also being less expensive?There's no difficulty at all with giving a cheaper product away if pricing is actually the issue. You're merely presenting another alternative that the other may or may not take. Always think about yourself and how you respond while you're buying stuff online.

If you want to click away from an offer, how many pop-up boxes can you endure before you grow frustrated? Internet marketers have all sorts of different opinions, but most ethical Internet marketers would agree that one or two pop-up boxes is acceptable, but past that point, there is an increasing possibility of frustration as the person visiting your website tries to exit but is continually blocked from doing so.

Imagine yourself in a shopping situation in which you chose not to purchase anything that day. Can you imagine if the salesperson blocked your passage to the door? How would you feel about the store's owner? That's precisely the sensation you do not want to have in the head of your prospective buyer. If someone wishes to click away from your offer, then you have to let them. If you block the door, you may lose a client for life.

Chapter 9: Give It Away

Sometimes the greatest way to earn a lifelong client is by giving away something for free. Remember that the free gift must be something of value. Everything you identify with your firm, whether via a relationship with another marketer or a free item on your website, must be of the highest quality. Customers will know quickly if you provide them with a "free" report that is practically useless, and that's the view they'll have of your organization.

Be as vigilant about the quality of your companions as you can. If you decide to establish a joint venture with other Internet marketers, one of the easiest methods to achieve this is by organizing a giveaway event during which each marketer provides something for free in return for traffic to his website.

People come to the Internet for knowledge, so a smart way to promote your company is by delivering useful material in an e-course that gives multiple messages over a period of time, such as a week or month. Free courses built on a succession of auto-responder messages are a terrific method to grow a list, but you must be sure – as always – to deliver on your prospective customers' expectations.

The material must be of excellent quality. Customers will expect that you will offer information about products that you have to sell, but you must be careful not to bombard them with sales messages. They signed up for material, and to keep up your half of the agreement, you must deliver them the material they asked for. It's all about creating your reputation as an Internet marketer of integrity, and everything you can do to expand their exposure to you will most certainly ensure their loyalty for a long time into the future.

In addition to free reports and e-courses, there are dozens of things you may give away: podcasts, webinars, video seminars, website evaluations, free samples of real items, etc. You're limited only by your creativity, as long as you make sure that the gift item complements your brand and delivers true value to your prospective buyer.

Conclusion

Internet marketing has modified the rules in many ways, yet the basics of selling have not changed over the years. Just remember to be yourself, cling to the greatest standards of ethics and integrity, and do for others what you would want them to do for you. If this is the paradigm through which you operate your company, you'll be well on your way to developing a successful, flourishing business for many years to come.

9 798848 126327